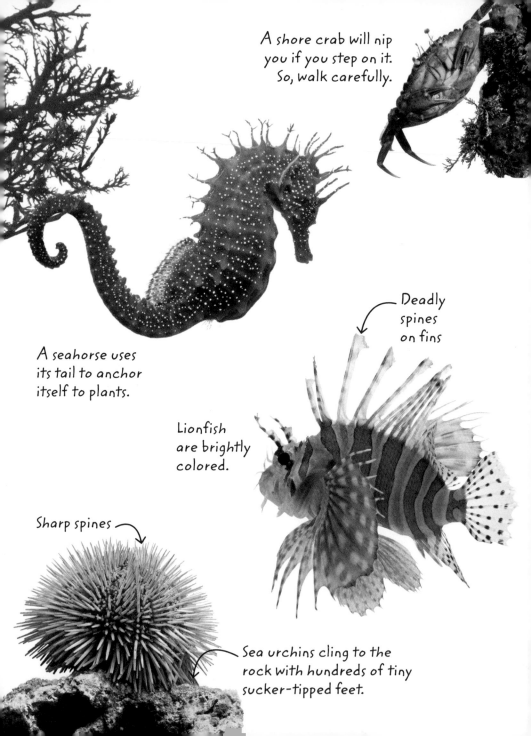

A shore crab will nip you if you step on it. So, walk carefully.

A seahorse uses its tail to anchor itself to plants.

Deadly spines on fins

Lionfish are brightly colored.

Sharp spines

Sea urchins cling to the rock with hundreds of tiny sucker-tipped feet.

Seashore

Written by David Burnie

Consultant: John Woodward

Penguin
Random
House

Senior editor Gill Pitts
Editors Radhika Haswani, Olivia Stanford
US Senior editor Margaret Parrish
Editorial assistance Cécile Landau
Senior art editor Ann Cannings
Art editor Kanika Kalra
Illustrators Abby Cook, Dan Crisp, Shahid Mahmood
Jacket co-ordinator Francesca Young
Jacket designers Dheeraj Arora, Amy Keast, Faith Nelson
DTP designers Sachin Singh, Dheeraj Singh

Picture researcher Sakshi Saluja
Senior producer, pre-production Nikoleta Parasaki
Producer Isabell Schart
Managing editors Soma B. Chowdhury,
Laura Gilbert, Monica Saigal
Managing art editors Neha Ahuja Chowdhry,
Diane Peyton Jones
Art director Martin Wilson
Publisher Sarah Larter
Publishing director Sophie Mitchell

Original Edition
Editor Claire Bampton
Art editor Rebecca Johns
Project editor Mary Ling
Production Catherine Semark
Editorial consultant Kathie Way
Illustrators Nick Hewetson, Tommy Swahn,
Peter Visscher
Picture researcher Diana Morris

First American Edition, 1994
This edition published in the United States in 2017 by
DK Publishing, 345 Hudson Street, New York, New York 10014

Copyright © 1994, 1997, 2017 Dorling Kindersley Limited
DK, a Division of Penguin Random House LLC
17 18 19 20 21 10 9 8 7 6 5 4 3 2 1
001–298587–Apr/2017

A catalog record for this book is available from the Library of Congress.
ISBN 978-1-4654-5756-1

DK books are available at special discounts when purchased in bulk for sales promotions, premiums, fund-raising, or educational use.
For details, contact: DK Publishing SpecialMarkets, 345 Hudson Street, New York, New York 10014 SpecialSales@dk.com

Printed and bound in China

The publisher would like to thank the following for their kind permission to reproduce their photographs:
(Key: a-above; b-below/bottom; c-center; f-far; l-left; r-right; t-top)
4 Dorling Kindersley: Natural History Museum, London (bl). **8 Dorling Kindersley:** Paul Wilkinson (cl). **8-9 Dorling Kindersley:** Stephen Oliver (t). **9 Dreamstime.com:**
Pockygallery11 (bl). **15 Dorling Kindersley:** Natural History Museum, London (cr). **18 Dreamstime.com:** Yael Weiss (tl). **22 Alamy Stock Photo:** David Pick (b). Dreamstime.
com: Mikelane45 (tr, cr). **23 Alamy Stock Photo:** Karen van der Zijden (b); ZUMA Press, Inc. (tl). **24 123RF.com:** guy ozenne (ca). **25 Getty Images:** Despite Straight Lines
(Paul Williams) (clb); Science Photo Library (cla). **26 Dreamstime.com:** Eugene Kalenkovich (bl). **27 Robert Harding Picture Library:** Frank Hecker / Okapia (br). **28
Dreamstime.com:** Mario Pesce (bl). **29 Alamy Stock Photo:** Blickwinkel / Hecker (cl). **34-35 Dorling Kindersley:** Natural History Museum, London (b). **39 Dorling
Kindersley:** Linda Pitkin (tl). **FLPA:** D P Wilson (r). **40 123RF.com:** Jolanta Wojcicka (bl). **41 123RF.com:** Krzysztof Odziomek (crb). **Dorling Kindersley:** Natural History
Museum, London (cla). **42 123RF.com:** Andrzej Tokarski (cl); Vitalii Hulai (cra). **43 Dorling Kindersley:** Jan Van Der Voort (crb). **45 Alamy Stock Photo:** Blickwinkel /
Hecker (br). **46 Dorling Kindersley:** Linda Pitkin (cr). Dreamstime.com: Asther Lau Choon Siew (tl). **47 123RF.com:** Sergdibrova (tl). **Dorling Kindersley:** Linda Pitkin (br).
54 Dorling Kindersley: Twan Leenders (br). **55 123RF.com:** Joe Quinn (c); Vasiliy Vishnevskiy (cra). **57 123RF.com:** Tiero (tl). **58-59 Alamy Stock Photo:** Carolyn Clarke
(b). **59 Alamy Stock Photo:** FLPA (cra). **Dreamstime.com:** Brett Critchley (cla). **Getty Images:** Glowimages (br)

Cover images: Front: 123RF.com: Vitalii Hulai (tc); Back: Dorling Kindersley: Natural History Museum, London (cla)

All other images © Dorling Kindersley
For further information see: www.dkimages.com

A WORLD OF IDEAS:
SEE ALL THERE IS TO KNOW
www.dk.com

Contents

The seashore

It's fun at the beach! In warm weather, it is a good place to keep cool, and there is always lots to do and see. In this book, you can find out about seashore plants and animals, and explore the different types of coast.

Exploring the shore
You can find out a lot about seashore wildlife without any equipment at all, but you will discover even more if you have a dip net.

Always ready
Some seashore animals are stuck to rocks, so they cannot run away. This makes them easy to study. Other animals are always on the alert for danger and will run or swim away if they see you coming.

Crabs scurry away sideways!

Hide and seek
Part of being a seashore explorer is knowing where to look for animals. This spiny squat lobster will hide under a stone when the tide is out.

Keeping a notebook

A notebook helps you to remember what you have seen on the shore. Drawing something is a good way of finding out exactly how it is shaped. You don't have to be a wildlife artist to keep a notebook, but with practice you might turn into one!

✳ Remember to record exactly where, and at what time of the year, the seashore animal was found. Always put animals back where you found them!

What shapes the shore?

The shore is always on the move. In some places, the sea eats away at the land, so the shore moves back. In other places, it builds up banks of sand or shingle, so the shore moves forward toward the sea. By knowing what to look for, you can see these changes at work.

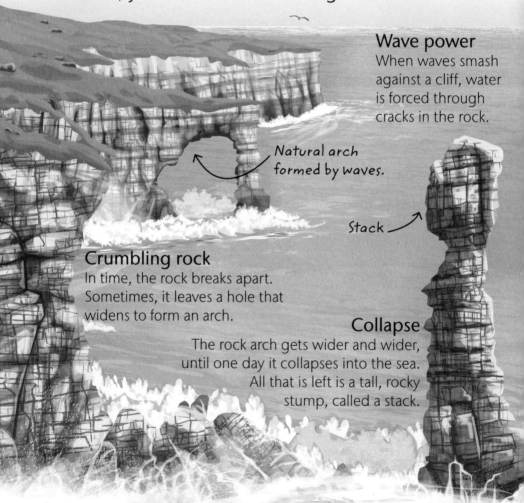

Wave power
When waves smash against a cliff, water is forced through cracks in the rock.

Natural arch formed by waves.

Stack

Crumbling rock
In time, the rock breaks apart. Sometimes, it leaves a hole that widens to form an arch.

Collapse
The rock arch gets wider and wider, until one day it collapses into the sea. All that is left is a tall, rocky stump, called a stack.

Graded grains

When the sea attacks a rocky shore it breaks up the rock and then pushes the pieces along the coast. It can move heavy boulders only a short distance, but it can carry sand a long way. The pebbles shown here were collected at regular intervals along a 12-mile (20-km) coastline.

Rocks are rounded into large pebbles by the pounding waves.

Large pebbles break up to make smaller ones.

Coarse pebbles are small enough to roll around in the waves.

The motion of the waves wears the pebbles away to shingle.

MAKING A SHORE PROFILE

If you draw part of a shoreline, you can see where the shore is changing. Cliffs and rocky stacks show where the shore is being eaten away. Level shingle and mud often show that the shore is building up.

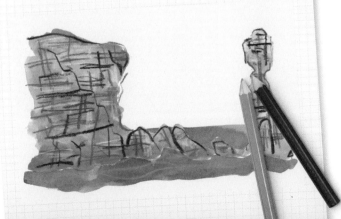

The pebbles eventually break up to make sand.

Making waves

Waves are made by the wind. When the wind blows over the ocean, it pushes and drags against the surface. The surface starts to ripple and waves form. Waves can travel huge distances. A storm can whip up waves in one part of an ocean, but many hours may pass before they reach the shore.

How waves work

If you watch a wave, the water seems to move forward. But if you float something on the water, you will find that it stays in more or less the same place. Each time the wave passes, the water actually moves in circles.

The circles are biggest near the surface and they get smaller deeper down.

Height of wave

Length of wave

How waves break

When waves approach the shore, they get taller and closer together. The bottom of each wave drags against the seabed and slows down, but the top of the wave keeps moving. Eventually, the surface topples over and crashes onto the beach.

Waves on the turn

Waves normally travel in straight lines. But if part of a wave enters shallow water, it slows down. The rest of the wave keeps moving as before, so the whole wave turns.

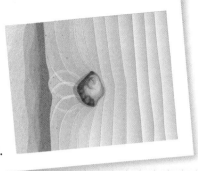

Here you can see how waves change direction as they pass an island. Behind the island the waves meet head on.

MAKING A PAPER BOAT

To make your own paper boat, you will need a square piece of paper.

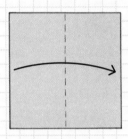

1. Fold the piece of paper in half.

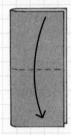

2. Fold the paper in half again, from top to bottom.

3. Fold the top sheet of paper backward to form a triangle.

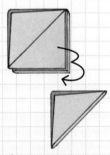

4. Fold the other three sheets of paper in the opposite direction.

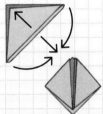

5. Pull open the triangle into a cup and fold it together to form a square.

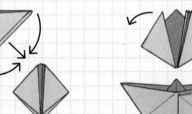

6. Gently pull out on the two halves to get your boat ready to sail.

Tides and tidal zones

The world's highest tides are found in the Bay of Fundy, between Canada and the United States. The sea level can rise or fall by the height of a four-story building in just six hours! However, even small tides have an important effect on shore wildlife.

When the sun and moon are in a line with the Earth, tides are extra high.

What causes tides?

Gravity causes tides. The sea is held in place by the Earth's gravity. The gravity of the sun and moon tugs at the Earth's seawater and pulls it toward them.

Zones on the shore

Some seashore animals and plants need to be in water all the time. Others can survive for a while in air, when the tide is out. This means that the wildlife is arranged in zones.

Oarweed grows in or below the lower shore.

Starfish usually live below the level of the lowest tide.

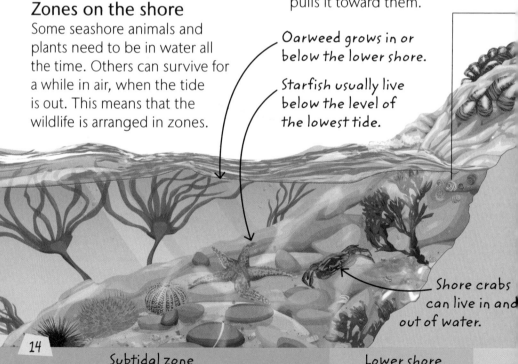

Shore crabs can live in and out of water.

Subtidal zone

Lower shore

Making a profile

On some shores, the zones are easy to see. You can keep a record of them by making a shore profile showing what kinds of plant and animal live at different levels. See if you can spot the very highest barnacle on a rocky shore.

Topshells live on the middle or lower shore.

Mussels close up at low tide to stop themselves from drying out.

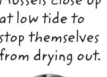

Sea lettuce grows in pools in the middle and upper shore.

Time for a meal

When the tide falls, many seashore birds come to the water's edge looking for small animals, stranded as the water level drops.

Oystercatchers use their long beaks to dislodge limpets.

Rock pipits feed all over the shore above water.

Periwinkles wander high into the splash zone.

Shrimp will die out of water.

Limpets can survive in air for a long time.

Middle shore   Upper shore   Splash zone

Signs in the sand

A sandy or muddy shore is a perfect place for spotting tracks. When the tide falls, it leaves a smooth, damp surface. Animal feet sink in as they walk over the sand or mud, leaving a tell-tale trail of footprints.

Gull tracks

A gull has three forward-pointing toes. The middle toe is straight, but the other two are curved. The toes are connected by flaps of skin called webs, which help the gull to swim.

A gull walks with its feet turned slightly inward.

Going for a run

A dog's paws have four small pads near the front and a larger pad at the back. If the dog is running, its claws leave deep marks in the sand.

Deep claw marks

Feet on the beach

The depth of your footprints, and the distance between them depend on how fast you are moving. When you look at footprints on the beach, see if you can figure out whether the person that left them was walking or running.

When someone is walking, the footprint is even.

Four-toed tracks

Cormorants usually live on rocks, but sometimes they leave tracks on sandy or muddy beaches. A cormorant foot has four outward-pointing toes, joined by a web of skin. All its toes are straight and the front toe is the longest.

Webbed toes

Heron tracks

Herons have three forward-pointing toes and one toe that points backward. They hunt by wading into the water and they often leave tracks on muddy sand. Herons have a long stride, so their footprints are wide apart.

Cormorants have short legs, so their footprints are close together.

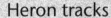

Backward-pointing toe

When someone is running, the toes leave more of a mark than the heels.

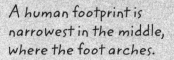

A human footprint is narrowest in the middle, where the foot arches.

Beach detective

Every day, the sea throws all kinds of objects onto the shore. These include shells, seaweed, and even old coins. For a beach detective, the best place to start investigating is the strandline—the line of "leftovers" washed up by the tide.

Hidden danger

The animals that live in these cone-shaped shells have powerful stings. Don't touch them!

Dead shells lose their color

A live starfish has flexible arms, but a dead one is stiff.

Stranded starfish

If a starfish is washed up on the beach, it will dry out and die. Its dry body then takes a long time to break down.

Driftwood often looks like bones or even animals.

Sea smooth

Pieces of wood are worn smooth by the sea.

Weed out of water

After a storm, seaweed is dislodged and thrown high up onto the beach. This bladderwrack has dried and become stiff.

Coral treasure

In warm parts of the world, you may see pieces of colorful coral.

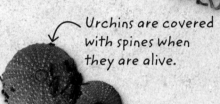

Urchins are covered with spines when they are alive.

Shell fragment

The sea keeps beach sand on the move and grinds up shells and stones.

Pieces of glass

No spines

Sea urchin shells are very fragile (weak) and they quickly get broken up by waves.

Cockle shells in two halves

Cone shell with short, pointed spine

Beach bones

Skulls are good for detective work, because they show how an animal lived. This skull belonged to a brown pelican that fished with its huge beak.

Long, flattened beak

Not everything on the beach is natural. Plastic does not decay in the sea and plastic bottles and bags can float across the oceans.

19

High and dry

For humans, cliffs can be dangerous places, so be careful when you go on a clifftop walk. However, for some animals, cliffs are places of safety. Seabirds breed on cliffs because their enemies cannot reach them there. For a few weeks every year, some sea cliffs are home to many noisy birds, jammed tightly together on every rocky ledge.

Miniature mine

A sandy, sheltered slope makes a perfect nest site for a cliff mining bee. The female bee digs out a branching tunnel. She stocks each side branch with some pollen and lays an egg in it.

Free flight

Gulls use the breeze over cliffs to lift themselves up, so they can stay in the air without flapping their wings. By adjusting the slant of its wings, a gull can hover and look for food.

Birdwatcher's paradise

Cliffs are wonderful places for birdwatching, particularly if you have a pair of binoculars. In spring and early summer, lots of birds set up home on different parts of the cliffs. In fall and winter, many birds leave for the open sea.

Clowns of the clifftops

It is easy to recognize a puffin, because it has a striped beak and bright red feet. Puffins nest in burrows, which they dig in clifftop turf. They often stand at the entrance to their burrows, cleaning their feathers and flapping their stubby wings.

Noisy neighbors

Kittiwakes nest on high rocky ledges. They make their nests from seaweed glued together with droppings. Kittiwakes often nest in huge numbers and their shrieking calls fill the air.

Life on a ledge

Guillemots do not make nests. Each female lays a single egg on a rocky ledge and stands guard over it. One end of the egg is very pointed, so that it can only roll around in a circle. This makes it less likely to fall over the edge.

Ground floor

Cormorants nest at the bottom of the cliffs, just above the waves. They lay eggs in seaweed nests. Cormorants often stand with their wings open, drying their feathers in the breeze.

Just visiting

In many parts of the world, the seashore is visited by different animals at different times of the year. In winter, many birds fly in from colder places far away. In spring and summer, the shore is a place where animals raise their young. Summer is also when humans flock to the coast for their vacations.

Summer visitors
Have fun at the seaside, and remember—when you go home, leave nothing behind but your footprints!

Pink-footed geese migrate along the coast.

Homing in
The coast is a good winter home for birds, as it is usually warmer than places farther inland.

Thief in the night
In warm parts of the world, the small Asian mongoose visits the shore after dark. It eats crabs and other seashore animals, and it also sniffs out turtle eggs buried in the sand. When it finds a turtle's nest, it digs up the eggs and feasts on them.

Fish out of water

The California grunion is a fish that lays its eggs on land. Grunion gather close to the shore after dark and then wriggle onto the beach to lay their eggs. As soon as the grunion have finished, they return to the sea.

Coming ashore to breed

Seals spend most of their time in water, but they give birth on land. Seals do not like to be close to humans. They come ashore on remote parts of the coast, where they can raise their young without being disturbed.

A seal pup may remain on shore for three months, before entering the sea.

Joining in

Dolphins are very clever animals that are full of curiosity. They often swim just in front of boats and enjoy playing with humans. In some parts of the world, dolphins come close to the shore to be near swimmers.

Dolphins are often friendly to humans.

Shell shapes

When you walk along a shore, you will find lots of empty shells. A shell is a special shelter that protects an animal from its enemies, and stops it drying out at low tide.

Cowries
A cowrie has a slit-shaped opening, lined with teeth like a comb.

Separated
Many shells have two hinged halves. After the owner dies, the two halves may soon become separated.

The top of the tightly coiled spire is the oldest part of this shell.

Olive shell
These shells look a bit like cones, but they are longer and thinner.

Wrap-around shell
A cone shell has an almost flat spiral at one end. The older the shell, the more turns its spiral has.

Corkscrew shell
Many shells have a long spiral at one end, like a corkscrew.

Inside of shell is smooth and shiny.

Smooth lining
Shells are often rough or bumpy on the outside, but inside they are usually very smooth.

The barnacles have a better chance of finding food if the shell's owner moves around.

This conch shell has been worn smooth by the sea.

Going to pieces
After a sea animal dies, its shell is slowly worn away. Eventually, only tiny pieces will be left.

Taken for a ride
The outside of a shell is often turned into a home by other animals or plants. Barnacles need a solid surface to live on and a shell suits them very well.

Seashells to keep
Shells like this scallop are fun to collect. Picking up empty shells does not harm wildlife, unlike buying shells in shops.

High rise
Slipper limpets grow in piles, with several shells stacked on top of each other.

It is worth sifting and sorting sand or shingle to find small shells like these for your collection.

Borers and burrowers

It's easy to dig a hole in the sand, but imagine being able to dig one through solid rock! Many seashore animals protect themselves by digging. Some live in rocks or wood, and others live in sand or mud.

Shell halves have rough edges.

Piddock's shell in rock

Burrowing in the sand

Tusk shells are mollusks that spend their lives in deep water, partly buried in sand. They collect food from the sand with their short tentacles. Their shells are often washed up on beaches.

Boring through rock

The two halves of the piddock's shell work just like a drill bit, turning one way and then the other, boring through soft rock.

Scraping out a home

Sea urchins use their spines and mouth parts to scrape a hollow shelter in solid rock. The spines are made of a mineral called calcite, which is similar to our teeth.

Sea urchins shelter in rock.

Hiding below the surface

Look carefully when you are walking at low tide for signs of worms below the surface. The sticky feeding tubes of the sand mason are easy to spot.

Waste piles up here.

Water, sand, and mud enter through one end.

Sand mason

U-tube

Mud and sand are perfect hiding places for animals with soft bodies. A lugworm lives in a U-shaped burrow. It swallows sand and mud that falls into the burrow's entrance, digesting any food that it contains. The lugworm then squirts waste out of the other end of the burrow.

Head

Tube of sand and small shells.

Lugworm's tail

Sinking the ship

Shipworms are not really worms at all, but mollusks. They use their shells to bore through wood, digesting wood flakes as they move along. When all boats were made of wood, shipworms were a serious pest.

Seashore fish

Many seashore animals stay in one place, so it is easy to get a close look at them. Watching fish is a bit more tricky. Fish are always on the alert and they will usually swim for cover if they see you coming.

Keeping upright

A seahorse is an unusual small fish that swims upright. Its body is covered with bony plates and it uses its tail to anchor itself to underwater plants. If you look at its head, you can see how it gets its name.

Fast mover

Blennies live in rock pools in many parts of the world. If you try to scoop one up with a net, you will find that it can change direction with lightning speed.

The butterfly blenny lives near the shore and in deep water.

Like most blennies, the tompot blenny has a long fin along the top of its body.

Finger-size fish

Gobies are small fish that nearly always live in shallow water. They have large eyes and are quick to spot any sign of danger. This is a black goby, which is common on rocky coasts.

Its paddle-shaped tail fin helps the goby to swim.

Sand-dweller

Dragonets bury themselves in sandy or muddy seabeds to hide from predators. They mostly eat worms, mollusks, and shellfish. Male dragonets are brightly colored, while females are a dull brown.

A splash of color

Many fish have dull colors, so they can hide easily. Instead of being drab, many wrasses are brilliantly colored. These two fish are cuckoo wrasses. The male and female look quite different.

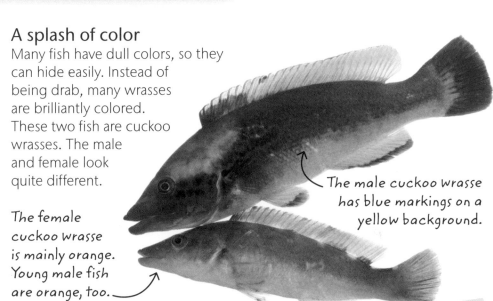

The male cuckoo wrasse has blue markings on a yellow background.

The female cuckoo wrasse is mainly orange. Young male fish are orange, too.

Look carefully

Life is not easy for seashore animals. They have to find enough to eat, but they also have to make sure that they do not get eaten themselves. Many avoid being seen by their enemies by having special shapes and colors that match their background.

Find that fish!

A pipefish has a very long body and is not much thicker than a pencil. It hides among underwater plants and sucks in pieces of floating food through its mouth.

Straight-nosed pipefish

You can only see the underside of a ray's body when it swims.

A perfect match

On the seabed there is nothing to hide behind. Flatfish and rays settle on the sand or gravel and have special markings that blend in with their background.

A sole is a type of flatfish. Can you spot the other one buried in the seabed?

This ray has brown and white markings that look like the sunlit seabed.

MAKING A SEASHORE MASK

To make your own disguise you will need a balloon, some newspaper, some sand, some shells, seaweed, half a cup of flour, and half a cup of water.

1. Mix flour and water to make a runny paste. Blow up the balloon. Glue layers of paper strips to the upper side of the balloon.

2. When the paper is hard and dry, lift the mask away from the balloon. If it is stuck, burst the balloon!

Wear the mask to disguise yourself.

3. Ask an adult to help you cut out some eyeholes and add some shells, sand, and seaweed.

Disappearing crab

The long-legged spider crab hides in seaweed and it even fastens small pieces to its body. Can you spot its claws and its long spidery legs?

Breathing tube of a buried masked crab

Underwater garden

One of the world's fastest-growing living things is giant kelp, a seaweed found off the coast of California. Seaweeds have flat fronds instead of leaves. They are useful hiding places for small fish. See how many you can find here!

Wracks often live in rock pools.

Brown seaweeds
Brown seaweeds grow at any depth. Wracks have narrow fronds. Kelps have broader fronds.

Green seaweeds

Green seaweeds grow all over the shore and even in salty pools above the tideline. Unlike brown seaweeds, they are quite flimsy. If you take a green seaweed out of the water it will collapse into a soggy mess.

Red seaweeds

All seaweeds need light to survive, but red seaweeds can live in places where the light is quite dim. They often grow in deep water, but you can also find them in pools.

Sugar kelp has fronds with crinkly edges.

Sea lettuce often lives near fresh water.

Kelps have a special anchor called a holdfast.

Red seaweed

Holding on

If you can imagine being out in a hurricane, you will know what it is like for seashore animals when the waves crash around them. Waves are very powerful and seashore plants and animals can only survive them by holding on tight. If they let go, they may be hurled against the rocks and torn to pieces.

A hanging egg

Dogfish are small sharks that lay their eggs close to the shore. Each egg has a rubbery case and special tendrils that wrap around seaweed. The tendrils hold the egg safely in place, while the young dogfish develops inside.

Stuck to a rock

Many rocky shore animals use special suckers to keep themselves in place. This sea anemone has fastened itself to a rock and extended its tentacles.

Sharp spines

Sea urchins cling to the rock with hundreds of tiny sucker-tipped feet.

Getting a grip

Seaweeds do not have proper roots, but they are good at holding on to rocks. Sometimes a seaweed fastens itself to a rock that is too small and light. If this happens, waves may pick up the rock and the seaweed and throw both of them onto the shore.

Crab on the move

The hermit crab uses its strong legs to hang on to rocks. If the crab is threatened, it often pulls its legs into its shell and drops into the safety of deeper water.

Sea anemone attached to hermit crab's shell

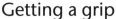

Hermit crab grips a rock.

Starfish cling on with tiny tube feet, just like sea urchins.

Riding on the storm

A limpet has a large, suckerlike foot that can clamp its shell on to the rock. Even powerful waves cannot budge it.

Limpet covered with algae

Life adrift

How many living things do you think there are in a bucket of seawater? About a dozen? A hundred? A single bucket of seawater can contain millions of living things. Together they make up "plankton"—a mass of life that drifts with the currents.

Fish fry
Cod release their eggs in the open sea and the eggs hatch into tiny "fry." Life is hard for these baby fish, and only a few survive.

When they hatch, cod fry feed on plankton.

Cased in glass
Diatoms are microscopic algae that float around in the sunlight. Each one is covered by a glasslike case.

Plantlike plankton
This strange plantlike object has long "horns" that help to stop it from sinking.

Changing shape
When crabs are young, they often drift in the open sea. As they get older, they change shape and live on the seabed.

Trailing by

Like most seaweeds, this kelp is fixed to
something solid on the seabed, so it cannot
move around. However, some seaweeds float
on the surface of the sea. They drift with the
currents and provide a home for tiny animals.

Drifting jellies

Jellyfish spend their lives
drifting with the tides and
currents. Once a jellyfish is
on land, its body collapses
and it cannot move at all.

*Long, feathery tentacles
carry food to its mouth.*

Slow progress

A jellyfish moves by
tightening and relaxing
its bell-shaped body.
When the bell tightens,
it pushes water
backward so that
the jellyfish moves
forward. Jellyfish cannot
swim very fast and they
often get washed up
on beaches.

Making a meal

In the sea, food is often all around. Most of this food is made of tiny particles that are smaller than a pinhead. Some seashore animals spend all their adult lives filtering out a share of this floating feast. Others get their food by hunting, or by bumping into it.

Eight-armed hunter

Octopuses hunt crabs and other small animals. An octopus will smother a crab with its long arms and then give the crab a venomous bite. Octopuses usually spend the day hidden in rocky crevices and they come out to feed after dark. They can change their skin color to match their background, or to show what mood they are in.

An octopus swims by squirting a jet of water out of the base of its body.

Powerful suckers allow the octopus to grip and move quickly over the seabed.

The living submarine

Cuttlefish are relatives of octopuses and they catch their prey using tentacles. Inside its body, a cuttlefish has a special shell containing lots of tiny spaces. It can fill the spaces with fluid or gas so that it rises or sinks, just like a submarine. It swims by rippling its fins, or by shooting out a jet of water.

Long hunting tentacles are surrounded by shorter arms to form a protective shield.

Danger adrift

The Portuguese man-of-war drifts on the surface of the sea and has long stinging tentacles that trail many yards into the water. If the tentacles touch a fish, they paralyze it and then pull it upward to be digested.

Filtering food

A sea squirt is a tiny animal shaped like a bottle with two openings. It sucks in water and filters out any particles of food. It then pumps the waste water out of the opening on its side.

Tentacles armed with thousands of tiny stings.

Water flows in here.

Water flows out here.

Sea squirts often live in groups.

39

Danger, keep clear!

When exploring the shore, remember that not everything likes to be touched or picked up. Most seashore animals are quite harmless, but some have sharp claws, or even venomous spines. A few have such powerful venom that they can kill or injure people.

Warning signs

Animals that are brightly colored, like this lionfish, are often dangerous. The lionfish lives in warm coral seas. Its stripes show that it has venomous spines. The lionfish's venom is strong enough to kill a human.

Deadly spines on fins

The fire coral's bright yellow color warns that it is dangerous.

Coral attack

All corals catch their prey by using stinging threads. The fire coral's threads can pierce human skin and cause a lot of pain.

Nasty nip

A shore crab will nip you with its pincers if you accidentally step on it. It might hurt, but some shore animals are much more dangerous.

Danger in the sand

The weever is a fish with venomous spines. It is hard to spot because it buries itself in the sandy seabed.

Venomous spines on fins

Deadly stone

Venomous tail spine

The stonefish is a relative of the lionfish and it also lives in the tropics. It lies on the seabed and snatches any smaller fish that pass by. The stonefish has small spines that can inject a deadly venom. People sometimes die from stepping on it by accident.

Sting in the tail

A stingray is named for the daggerlike venomous spines in its long tail. When it senses danger, it flicks its tail to attack.

41

Life in the dunes

When sand is dry, it is easily carried about by the wind. If the wind blows steadily from the sea to the land, it often pushes the sand into piles called sand dunes. Dunes have their own special wildlife. See the change as you walk inland from the sea.

Feeding by night

Snails that live on dunes feed mainly at night. During the day, they stay inside their shells to stop their bodies from drying out.

Feeding by day

You can often see sand lizards sunbathing before setting off to hunt. They get their energy from the warmth of the sun. The lizards then scuttle over the sand in search of small insects.

Changing landscape

The part of the dune nearest the sea is usually made of bare, shifting sand. Farther away from the sea, grasses begin to take root and they hold the sand grains together.

Sea lyme grass is a plant that can live on the seaward edge of dunes.

MAKING SAND MOVE

In this project, you can see how wind keeps sand grains on the move.

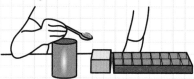

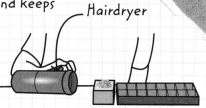
Hairdryer

1. Put a block of wood next to an empty ice-cube tray. Now make a small "dune" by piling sand onto the block.

2. Make a wind blow sideways across the "dune," either by blowing through a straw or by holding a hairdryer close to the sand.

3. The sand in the "dune" will be carried sideways by the wind. The heaviest grains will not travel far, but lighter ones may reach the end of the tray.

Damp hollows called dune slacks make a home for animals like this natterjack toad.

Marram grass is important to most dunes. It has long roots that stop the sand from moving.

The red-and-black cinnabar moth is often seen feeding from plants in the dunes.

Sandy shore

Sand is soft to walk on and it is easy to dig up and play with. Have you ever wondered exactly what sand is, or how it is made? To find out about sand, you will need to look very closely.

Volcanic sand
This sand is made from rock from a volcano. The sea grinds it down into a black sand.

Mineral sand
This forms when the sea grinds down solid rock. It contains silica, a substance used to make glass.

Glued by water
Sandcastles are made from millions of grains of damp sand. When you build a sandcastle, the water that surrounds each grain of sand works like glue and holds the sandcastle together. If the sand dries out, the castle soon falls down.

Shell sand
This sand is made from tiny pieces of shell. Damp shell sand sticks to skin, because most of it is flat.

MAKING A SAND TRAY

You can start your own sand collection by making this special cardboard tray. Let the sand dry out before you add it to your collection.

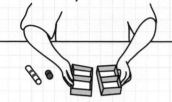

1. Glue four small cardboard boxes together, side-by-side.

2. Carefully cut out cardboard for labels. Fold them in half and glue them to one wall of each section.

3. Now pour your sand into each section of the display case.

Fine-grained sand made of light-colored rock

Fine-grained sand made of gray-layered rock

Very coarse sand made of volcanic rock

Coarse sand made of broken pieces of shell and coral

Jumping to safety

If you walk along a sandy beach, you may notice clouds of tiny animals jumping out of your way. These are sand hoppers—small relatives of shrimps and lobsters. They feed on rotting seaweed and jump by flicking their tails.

Coastal corals

Corals are small animals that often live close together. Many protect themselves by building hard cases. As the coral animals grow and then die, their cases pile up and can form huge banks called coral reefs.

Mushroom coral

This coral contains just one polyp (coral animal), protected by a stony cup that looks like part of a mushroom. It is not fixed to the seabed. If it is turned over, it can slowly pull itself the right way up.

Coming out to feed

These polyps are trailing their tentacles in the water to catch food. Their tentacles have tiny stinging threads that shoot out when a small animal brushes past them.

If a large animal comes close, the polyps quickly pull in their tentacles.

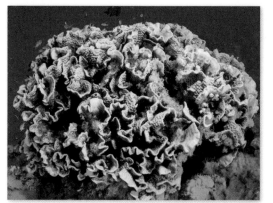

Cabbage coral

This cabbage coral looks very much like a plant, but each of its "leaves" is made up of hundreds of tiny coral animals living close together. Cabbage corals live near the surface, where the water is sometimes rough.

As cabbage corals grow and die, they help to build coral reefs.

Coral fans

Sea fans often grow in deep water and can be more than 10 ft (3 m) long. They do not have a hard casing and so can bend quite easily. Sea fans usually grow at right angles to the current. This gives them the best chance of catching any food that is drifting past. A large sea fan is often home to many other living things, including crabs, sponges, and barnacles.

The spreading shape of this purple sea fan shows that it is growing in calm water.

47

Shingle beach

Shingle beaches are made up of lots of small, rounded stones. They are difficult places for plants and animals to live because the sea keeps the stones on the move. A lot of the wildlife on a shingle beach lives high up on the shore, beyond the reach of the waves.

Searching for water

Shingle is full of air spaces and does not hold water. Plants that live on shingle need very long roots, so that they can reach the water far below the surface. They also need tough leaves, so they can cope with strong winds.

Sea holly has hard, prickly leaves.

Terns are small gulls.

Sea campion grows in round clumps.

The sea pea is one of the few plants that can live on open shingle banks.

Hidden on the beach

You might think that it is hard to hide on shingle. However, small birds like the ringed plover hide away by looking just like stones.

Disappearing eggs

Terns lay their eggs in hollows on a shingle bank. Their eggs are speckled, which makes them very hard to see against the surrounding stones.

Tern's eggs

A tern feeds by hovering above the water and then splashing down to catch small fish.

Oystercatchers are noisy birds with beaks like hammers, which they use to smash open shells.

The yellow horned poppy grows seeds in a long pod.

Sanderling

Rock pipit

The ringed plover feeds close to the water.

49

Rocky shore

For many plants and animals, a rocky shore makes an ideal place to live. Unlike shingle, solid rock does not get dragged around by the waves. Small plants and animals can live on the rocks, without being battered to pieces or swept away.

Layers of life

The best time to explore a rocky shore is at low tide. Some barnacles and winkles can survive out of water for a long time, so they can live high up on the rocks. Other sea animals, such as sea squirts and starfish, need to stay damp.

The turnstone scuttles over rocks, looking for small animals.

Lichens live on bare rock, just beyond the reach of waves. They grow very slowly, but live for a long time.

Sea squirts

Brittlestar

Life from long ago

Rocky shores can be very good places for fossil hunting. Fossils are the remains of plants or animals that have slowly turned to stone. This fossil is of an ammonite. Ammonites were common more than 66 million years ago.

Thrift grows on rocky ledges close to the sea. Its tough leaves are not harmed by salty spray from the waves.

Wild carrot grows in dry ground on cliff tops. Garden carrots are close relatives of this plant.

Rock samphire has fleshy leaves that store water.

Bootlace worms can be over 16 ft (5 m) long.

Sea anemones live close to the low-tide mark. They pull in their tentacles if the tide leaves them in the open air.

Winkles clamp themselves to the rock at low tide.

Rock pool

When the tide falls, most of the shore is left high and dry. In a rock pool, however, some plants and animals can stay safely underwater until the sea returns. Every rock pool is different—shallow pools sometimes have only a few plants or animals, but deeper ones may be packed with life.

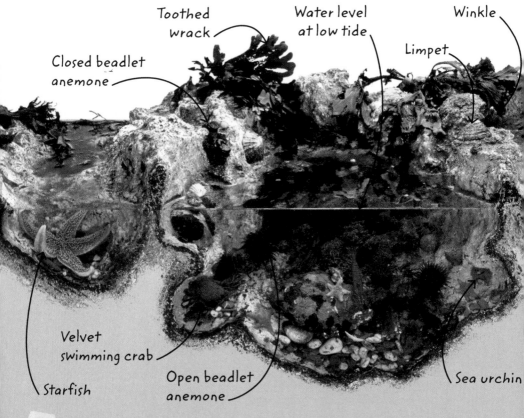

Toothed wrack

Water level at low tide

Winkle

Limpet

Closed beadlet anemone

Velvet swimming crab

Starfish

Open beadlet anemone

Sea urchin

MAKE A ROCK POOL VIEWER

Rock pools are fascinating places to explore. Ask an adult to help you make this rock pool viewer, so you can get a clear look at the animals in the pools without disturbing them.

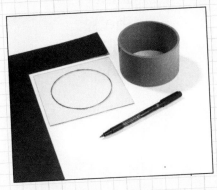

1. Cut a piece of plastic tube about 4 in (10 cm) long. Trace around one end on a piece of clear plastic.

2. Cut out the plastic circle with scissors. Use sandpaper to sand the edges of the tube. Glue the piece of plastic to one end of the tube.

 Be careful when visiting rock pools—wet rocks and seaweed can be very slippery. Also, watch out for the in-coming tide!

3. Once the glue has dried, your viewer is ready to use. Just push the plastic end into the water and take a look.

Muddy shore and salt marsh

You won't find people lazing around on a muddy beach or soaking up the sunshine in a salt marsh. For some plants and animals, though, a muddy shore is the perfect home. Although the mud is salty, it is also rich in nutrients and full of life.

Glass from plants

Glasswort is a short, fleshy plant that lives close to the water's edge. Long ago, people collected glasswort and burned it because its ashes can be used to make glass.

Glasswort has fat, rounded stems and tiny leaves.

Sea aster

Marsh flowers

Like many salt marsh plants, sea aster flowers late in the summer. It grows away from the water's edge.

A painted lady butterfly drinks nectar from sea aster flowers.

Seaside terrapin

Most terrapins live in fresh water, but the American diamondback lives in salty water near the coast. It feeds at night and often spends the day basking in the sunshine.

Sea spurrey flowers close up quickly if the sun goes in.

Sea purslane has small yellow flowers. It lives at the inland edge of salt marshes, where the ground is drier.

Teal fly over marshes in winter to look for food.

Lying in wait
A heron hunts by stealth. It wades into the water and then stands absolutely still. If a fish swims past, the heron stabs at it with its sharp beak.

Cord grass grows in wet, salty mud. It stops the mud from being washed away and helps to turn it into dry land.

Beauty in the marsh
Sea lavender has lots of small but brightly colored flowers, and in late summer it often turns whole marshes purple. The flowers keep their color if they are picked and left to dry out.

Sea plantain has narrow, leathery leaves and tiny flowers in long clusters.

Mangrove swamp

In warm parts of the world, muddy coasts are often covered by mangrove trees. Their spreading roots stop the mud from being washed away. A mangrove swamp is a jungle that is flooded with seawater at high tide and has its own special wildlife. Animals live in the mud, on the roots, and clamber among the branches.

Stick in the mud

Mangroves are unusual trees, because they can grow in salty water. They have special roots that anchor them in the mud and breathing roots that collect air.

Fish out of water

Mudskippers are finger-size fish that can breathe air. They use their stumpy fins to climb up mangrove roots. When danger threatens, they hop back into the water.

Mudskipper clinging to a root.

Mangrove prop roots are anchored in mud.

Getting the message

At low tide tiny fiddler crabs come out of their mud burrows to search for food. Males have one especially large claw that they wave to attract mates.

Spread out to dry

Anhingas, or snake birds, live in the swamps of the southern United States. They feed on fish and swim with just their heads and snakelike necks above the surface. After each fishing expedition, an anhinga spreads out its wings to dry.

Feathers dry in the sunshine.

Living on leaves

Mangrove leaves are tough and leathery, but for the proboscis monkey they are an important source of food. These rare monkeys live in mangrove swamps on the island of Borneo. Male proboscis monkeys are twice as big as the females and their noses are much larger.

Harbor and pier

A harbor is a busy place, where boats are tied up and fish are brought to the shore. Harbor walls are usually made of rock, concrete, or wood. Below the high-tide mark, tiny plants and animals settle, and soon the harbor wall is full of life.

Keeping things clean

In busy harbors, the water can easily become polluted. This makes it difficult for sea animals to survive. If the water is clean, a harbor can be home to many different kinds of fish.

Many harbors have rivers flowing into them. The water in harbors is less salty than water in the open sea.

Fighting for food

Gulls are nature's scavengers.
They eat almost anything, from
crabs and dead fish, to fries
and sandwiches.

Sea slaters hide during
the day. At night they
look for scraps
of food.

Top of the pile

Wooden pilings are home
to many small animals and
plants. At low tide some
of these are easy to see.

Sea anemone

Mussels grow like
bunches of grapes
on wood or rocks.

Index

Acknowledgments

**Dorling Kindersley
would like to thank:**

Robin James and Mike
Quarm from Weymouth
Sealife Centre.
Tina Robinson, Susan
St. Louis, Shakera Mangera,
Mark Haygarth, and Faith Nelson
for design assistance.
Gemma Ching-A-Sue and
Alison Owen for modeling.
Hilary Bird for indexing.

Starfish